Western Steam Days Remembered II

Strathwood

Western Steam Days Remembered II

Front Cover: Stand well back as 7003 Elmley Castle roars over Goring troughs with her scoop down to pick up water on 4 November 1961, with this morning's up Cheltenham Spa Express. *Colour Rail*

Strathwood

Western Steam Days Remembered II

A selection of some of the essential books and magazines from the era along with a few other reminders of the locomotives.

First published 2019

ISBN 978-1-913390-00-6

Copyright Strathwood Publishing 2019
Published by Strathwood Publishing, 9 Boswell Crescent, Inverness, IV2 3ET
Telephone 01463 234004
Printed by Akcent Media

Contents
                                    Page

Preface

Having been asked about completing some follow on Western Region Steam Days Remembered albums after the release of the first during 2013, having been so well received at its launch, the second and third volumes being released together now are perhaps well overdue, after such a wait.

It was planned to release this second volume a number of years ago, so to those of you who have been patiently waiting for its release with kind words of encouragement, I thank you.

My personal memories of Western Region steam are a little thin involving severely run down and filthy locomotives from the long footbridge that gave access to the shed at Southall, not that as a young school boy back then I was ever going to dare to bunk the shed. Another of life's opportunities missed sadly.

One of those who has done so much to help preserve and make available photographer's collections is John Chalcraft the founder of Rail Photoprints. A few years ago I asked John to set down some of his own personal railway recollections from his youth. Having been guilty of sitting on these notes for a while I am sure the release of this title will bring a pleasant surprise.

We will all have our favorites from the past, I hope you will enjoy this compilation and we must also thank the foresight of the photographers and the kindness of those who have allowed their work to be seen and appreciated by a wider audience.

Kevin Derrick
Inverness 2019

Below: From a vantage point by the Mitre Bridge taking the West London goods lines across the entrance point to Old Oak Common's carriage sidings on 19 October 1963, we see the arrival of the eleven year old Robert Stephenson & Hawthorn built pannier 8481, with another rake from Paddington, if we look carefully we can see a maroon Western diesel tucked in at the rear to reduce line occupation for light engine movements. *Colour Rail*

Introduction - Steam around Bath

Born and bred in Bath the first 18 months of life were spent on the opposite side of the River Avon just 75 yards from Bath Green Park, it was no wonder that I became entranced by the railway.

Family tales of my childhood indicate that I was a fractious child unless in sight of a railway and apparently it was a regular thing for me to be taken to Bath Spa station to see the Bristolian drop its slip coaches, all of that just to shut me up. Another story related to my Mother receiving wolf whistles when on one occasion she was dragged into

Bath Green Park shed by her 6 year old son. A later move found the family living at Twerton and I could hear (but not see) the trains leaving the tunnel, needless to say it was not long before little Johnny went missing only to be found sat in the field next to the tunnel entrance a place where I spent many hours.

I used to visit the tunnel mouth at every opportunity even before school the main attraction at 08.00 in the morning being the '100' express so remembered for the Western Region reporting number, a regular working for a Laira based Castle but on one occasion in 1955 it had 70015 Apollo in charge. Summer evenings were spent 'guess where' the attraction being the evening 'trials' working from Swindon. The rarest combination on the service I can remember being a Grange double headed with 0-6-2T 6666, and in early 1960, D6305 and D6306 were seen on the working.

School holidays were spent sitting on the platform at Bath Spa, anxiously peering through the windows of a stopping service to identify the Radyr 72xx 2-8-2T that always seemed to run down the through road (at that time Bath Spa had two through lines) with a Radyr – Salisbury coal working. Occasionally I was able to scrounge a lift across to Bristol Temple Meads where new wonders were seen. The regularly double headed 'Devonian' with its Jubilee/Black 5 combination always excited and on one occasion Unrebuilt Patriot 45508 (with stovepipe chimney) turned up - a real scoop as it was allocated to Carlisle Upperby.

My first trip to Swindon Works was on a Wednesday afternoon in July 1958 (at the time there was a weekly works visit on Wednesdays), the visit produced 18000, and 9Fs 92195 – 92200 all in various stages of construction plus numerous Castles and Kings. Shortly afterwards it was found out that on Sundays a Swindon Works Permit also normally got a trip round 82C and the scrapyard, from that point on-wards Sunday became the day to visit the works, the note on the permit that all participants should be 16 years of age was, of course, ignored – I was 12 but nobody seemed to check.

Early 1960, found me on a school organized trip to London, hauled by Castle 5076 Gladiator I arrived at Paddington somewhat dirtier than many of my compatriots having been window hanging for most of the

Above: Pride of the much lamented Somerset & Dorset Railway were their 2-8-0s such as 53810 which was the regular train engine at the time, it passes Bath Junction as it runs into Bath Green Park with the 10.42 (So) Exmouth to Cleethorpes service, on 4 August 1962. *Rail Photoprints*

trip, after all I wasn't going to miss anything Schools 30908 Westminster, D8004 and D601 Ark Royal all found their way into the book before we made our way to Camden, Willesden, Old Oak Common, Cricklewood and Kentish Town, I still remember my first sight at Camden as we walked over the footbridge with 46146 The Rifle Brigade and 46245 City of London simmering on the back road beneath us.

After that the Bristol area seemed somewhat mundane but my weekly pocket money used to purchase a day return ticket from Bath Green Park to Bristol Temple Meads the Midland route being the preferred option as it meant passing Bath Green Park and Bristol Barrow Road with the chance of some cops, power was normally one of Bath's three Ivatt 2-6-2Ts 41241 – 41243, other highlights would normally be the Barrow Road Patriots or possibly a Holbeck Jubilee among other bits.

Christmas 1960, saw me become the proud owner of my first camera, a plastic bodied Brownie 127 with a shutter offering 1/50th second,

surprisingly one or two reasonable negs still exist my first photo being County 1009 at Bath Spa station. The Brownie lasted two years before it was replaced with a Halina 35X which cost the princely sum of £7.13.3 from my hard earned paper round money, the problem then was do I spend money on film and developing and forego trips or was the notebook full of numbers more important, to my regret I chose the latter.

September 1962, saw a trip to Blackpool for the illuminations with my parents, B1 61369 was photographed on Blackpool Central station amid a procession of Black 5s and Jubilees, on the Saturday I made the mistake of lending my parents the camera while I visited Preston and missed photographing five Coronations and twelve Jubilees – big mistake!

My regular trips to Swindon meant that I witnessed the final building of the 9Fs culminating in Evening Star, and at the same time alongside steam construction Swindon was building the Class 42 Warships, construction of the Westerns commenced as the last Warships were complete, but it was the closure of Bristol Bath Road to steam in September 1960 and its subsequent rebuilding as a diesel depot re-opening in May 1961 which really indicated that steam was on its way out.

During Saturdays in 1961 and 1962, Bath Green Park was always an attraction with the S & D line cross country services which despite the allocation of 9Fs 92203 – 92206 continued to provide the spectacle of double headed passenger services for the

Left: A visit to Swindon Works on 6 September 1959, rewards us with a view of an ex-works Churchward designed 2-8-0 4703, here awaiting a return to its home shed of 82B St. Philips Marsh in Bristol. *Gerald T. Robinson*

climb over the Mendips. The variety of locomotive classes also increased with regular appearances of Scots, Patriots and the occasional B1, but even before the Pines Express was moved away from the route in September 1962, the specter of dieselisation had arrived with a regular Peak working, the loco then being used on a Bath – Bristol local for refueling purposes before it returned to Bath to take a northbound working. Once the Pines had been re-routed the death knell for the S & D was sounding, culminating in the lines closure in March 1966. However, even during the run down it still produced the occasional surprise but when filthy Crewe North Britannia 70034 turned up it was exceptional, to my knowledge the only 'Brit' to visit Green Park.

During 1961 I saw my first brush with the British Transport Police, the local spotters at Bath Green Park used to congregate on a waste mound at the entrance to Bath Midland Goods, where we used to watch the comings and goings, it had the benefit of giving a clear view of any freight movements, all comings and goings from the shed and Green Park station. Up to thirty of us would be there on a good Saturday, minding our own business but always mindful that we should stay on our side of the signal wires and cabling, we were accepted as part of the railway scene by local railway men (and why not), then one summer morning the British Transport Police arrived, the normal interrogation occurred – what were we doing (wasn't it obvious), why were we on the track (we weren't) and finally names were taken. This was the prelude to several further police raids normally about 12.00 as the 'Pines' rolled in. Not a lot seems to have changed over the years instead of using the harmless railway enthusiast as 'eyes and ears' we continue to be harassed by security and the 'jobsworths' of the railway industry, many of whom are totally oblivious to the official guidelines and view the enthusiast armed with camera and notebook as terrorist potential.

With the closure of 82A Bath Road to steam the Western Region steam servicing was undertaken at St. Philips Marsh, to the joy of local enthusiasts as 82B was considerably easier to bunk than 82A had been. Once the visit to 82B was accomplished then a 25 minute walk took you to Barrow Road, where entrance to the shed was normally accomplished over the wall at the Bristol end of the shed, that was fine until the Shed Foreman decided to use old lubricating oil on the top of the wall resulting in numerous pairs of spoilt trousers, but it was normally a risk worth taking. Then in June 1964 the closure of St. Philips Marsh and all Bristol area steam servicing was then undertaken at Barrow Road, closure of the latter occurred in 20 November 1965 leaving Bath Green Park the only steam servicing facility in my area.

Right: Dressed in a filthy black workaday livery the 1949 built Hawksworth designed pannier 1506 enjoys the winter sunshine at Ebbw Junction on 19 February 1961. *Gerald T. Robinson*

The end of steam in the Bristol area meant that I had to travel further for my 'fix', day trips to the Southern were the shortest distance so Southampton became a regular destination but trips to Leeds, York, and of course the Manchester area were commonplace. The growing scrapyard at Barry was also a regular destination, throughout the 1960s many locomotive convoys from throughout England made their way to this spotting heaven, and many 'cops' were found there, the fact that by that time they were rusting, lifeless hulks meant nothing, they were still a line in the book!

When 1968 came and steam became confined to an enclave in the North West Patricroft, Bolton, Lostock Hall, Rose Grove, and Carnforth were meccas for the enthusiast as steam numbers steadily reduced until we reached 4 August which was the day steam officially ended (ignoring the special of the 15 Guinea special which ran on 11 August). That August weekend hundreds (if not thousands) made the pilgrimage north to witness the passing of an era, many of them including myself ended up on the tracks, signals, bridge abutments etc at Blackburn, the operating authorities must have had a nightmare but police presence was low key, the weather was kind, we got our photos and went home albeit with a feeling of melancholy, our worlds would never be the same again.

Then, realization, there was still operational steam in small enclaves throughout the country as small steam locomotives were in operation in industry, APCM Swanscombe, NCB Mountain Ash, BSC Corby, to name but a few all became tourist destinations. Also just a Hovercraft journey away (from Ramsgate) the SNCF still operated Steam at Calais and Boulogne the next 5 years were spent in some of the most obscure destinations possible or visiting the continent. Then in 1974, somebody mentioned that the 'Westerns' were finishing this re-ignited the interest in the British Railway scene and with a growing liking for the Class 50s my love of the UK railway scene returned. Sadly it was to die 'the death' after privatisation when the Class 66 was introduced and our trusty UK built locomotives were largely eliminated.

John Chalcraft
Rail Photoprints
Bristol

Opposite: The pride of Swindon's loyal workforce shows as 6011 King James I awaits a return to service after a brief visit to the works here in February 1962. *Gerald T. Robinson*

Above: The nameplate and splasher of 5031 Totnes Castle appears to have enjoyed a recent wipe over from an oily rag, although the boiler casing suggests a lack of cleaners at her home shed of 84A Stafford Road on 28 July 1963. *Colour Rail*

A Visit to Swindon

Opposite: Taking a stroll through the roundhouse at Swindon on 12 November 1961, we are rewarded with a trio of Castles in company of a Hall and an ex-works 1008 County of Cardigan. *Colour Rail*

In September 1955, this brand new Standard Class 4MT 4-6-0 75069 was just days out of Swindon Works for testing before being fitted with 74C Dover Marine shedplate upon her delivery to Southern Region shed. *Colour Rail*

Opposite: The brutal elegance of Collett's 1937 rebuild of the 2-8-0T 4239 into a 2-8-2T shows. Renumbered as 7240 she stands ex-works and ready for traffic once more at her home shed of 86A Ebbw Junction, outside Swindon Works on 17 June 1962. *Strathwood Library Collection*

On 6 May 1956, the ex-works 1022 County of Northampton stands outside the works in steam ready for a running in duty, most likely on a Swindon to Didcot stopping service, before a return to duty out of 84K Chester. *Colour Rail*

Another of Hawksworth's designs were the lightweight 1600 Class 0-6-0PTs, this freshly built example 1662 was being put to good first use as one of the works shunters on 13 March 1955 before being released to take up service at 85A Worcester as her first shed. *Colour Rail*

Opposite: Outside the works on 26 March 1961, was this oddball combination of the sparkling 6953 Leighton Hall temporarily stabled with an un-lined green Class 2MT mogul tender. This works visit would see the Collett designed Hall through to withdrawal in December 1965. *Colour Rail*

Opposite: A duo of Swindon built Standards, with Class 9F 92208 from 88A Cardiff Canton and Class 4MT 75022 from 81F Oxford, as they appear to be ready to undergo running in before a return to their home sheds on 24 June 1962. *C. H. Gooch/Railway Images*

On 6 October 1963, pannier tank 3605 from 84B Oxley shed serves a spell running in as 82C Swindon shed's yard pilot. However, someone will need to change that shed plate as Oxley's code had changed to 2B while she was in the works. *Rail Online*

East meets west in Swindon's shed yard as this Thompson Class B1 from 2F Woodford Halse is ready to depart, as the crew onboard 61039 Steinbok take instructions from the yard foreman. *Colour Rail*

The new order may be in the background outside Swindon Works in April 1962, but evidence of the old guard still shows on the tender of the Churchward mogul 6324, in steam just now but about to be withdrawn imminently the same month. *Colour Rail*

The safety valves are beginning to sizzle onboard 5943 Elmdon Hall as she keeps company with a Castle on her home shed of 82C Swindon during April 1962. Paired at this point with a Hawksworth tender she would be withdrawn in June the following year. *Colour Rail*

Opposite: Not a bad spot to take lunch in order to keep an eye on anything passing the works sat alongside an Ivatt Class 4MT which has arrived for repairs during the summer of 1964. Standing behind is another tender from a second class member here today as well, both carry a single line tablet recess. *Strathwood Library Collection*

Opposite: Finally back out into the sunshine late in 1957 for Cardiff Canton's Britannia 70025 Western Star, having arrived here at Swindon Works at the end of April 1957 for a General Overhaul, this was reported to have taken six months to complete. During this time, the boiler was lifted, the smoke deflectors were modified to Swindon's specifications after the Didcot accident with 70026 Polar Star on 20 November 1955, which was blamed upon the original handrails fitted to the smoke deflectors interfering with the driver's view of signals. *Colour Rail*

Taken earlier on 24 April the same year as the Didcot tragedy, the newly arrived Churchward 0-6-0ST 1365 from Plymouth's Laira shed has just begun work as a shed pilot here at Swindon. It would stay in residence until June 1961 when a move to St. Phillips Marsh was made, seventeen months prior to it being withdrawn in November 1962. It was then to travel to Cashmore's scrapyard in Newport for breaking up in September 1963. *Colour Rail*

In Service with a King

The latest Hymek diesel arrivals were closing in around 6018 King Henry VI in Swindon's shed yard on 28 April 1963, as her crew take a breather during the Stephenson Locomotive Society's Farewell to the Kings railtour to allow participants to visit the works. *RCTS Collection*

Opposite: Happier times just a couple of years beforehand, as 6015 King Richard III receives a little bit of tender care with the oil can at Leamington from her crew, meanwhile the King's boiler begins to show impatience to resume the journey. *Colour Rail*

A dramatic appearance onto Goring's water troughs for 6019 King Henry V at the head of the up Red Dragon on 4 March 1961. This magnificent King was based out of 88A Cardiff Canton, this service will have left Swansea just before 09.00 and was timed to arrive at Paddington just after 13.00, stopping only at Cardiff and Newport. *Colour Rail*

Opposite: It will soon be departure time at Paddington for 6002 King William IV, the fireman has the pep pipe hanging over the side, having no doubt tidied up the footplate ready for the off. Alongside one of Old Oak Common's, Hawksworth designed panniers awaits release carrying the pilot duty number of 6 today. *Colour Rail*

The Western Region also favoured large reporting numbers to help staff to identify trains in the working timetable en-route, such as here on 6015 King Richard III storming comfortably along near Beaconsfield. *Colour Rail*

Opposite: Whereas 6003 King George VI makes easy work of its nine coaches, on this up service heading away from Sonning Cutting on 30 April 1960, absolutely nothing to do with James Bond. *Colour Rail*

Opposite: The 81A Old Oak Common smoke box shed plate is absent from 6005 King George II, as it sweeps past Reading West on 27 October 1962, with a special just weeks before being withdrawn. *Colour Rail*

A young fireman looks longingly upon 6022 King Edward III at Old Oak Common in September 1962, once again days before its withdrawal from service. The fireman might want to think twice though looking at a tender full of ovoids rather than best Welsh coal. *Colour Rail*

A view back through Hatton station, as 6027 King Richard I sweeps majestically through during June 1960 whilst based out of 84A Stafford Road. Between December 1958 and its withdrawal in September 1962, this locomotive was re-allocated eight times, back at forth between Laira, Stafford Road and Old Oak Common. *Colour Rail*

Opposite: Accelerating hard near Cardiff in the late 1950s, we find 6004 King George III. The Kings were four-cylinder locomotives designed and built to the maximum weight allowed on the former GWR's mainlines, making the class of thirty engines the most powerful in the UK when built between 1927 and 1930. All of the class were fitted with four-row high temperature superheaters and mechanical lubricators from 1947, their performance was improved once more after 1955, when they were all fitted with double chimneys. *Colour Rail*

An ex-works 6010 King Charles I, still carrying a single chimney and the old emblem arrives at Corsham with a running in turn around 1956. The leading coach is a Dean designed vehicle now in use for the weekly stores delivery to station and signal box staff. *Colour Rail*

Now with a double chimney and looking more out of favour, 6010 King Charles I brings a morning extra through Goring on a crisp 4 November 1961. *Colour Rail*

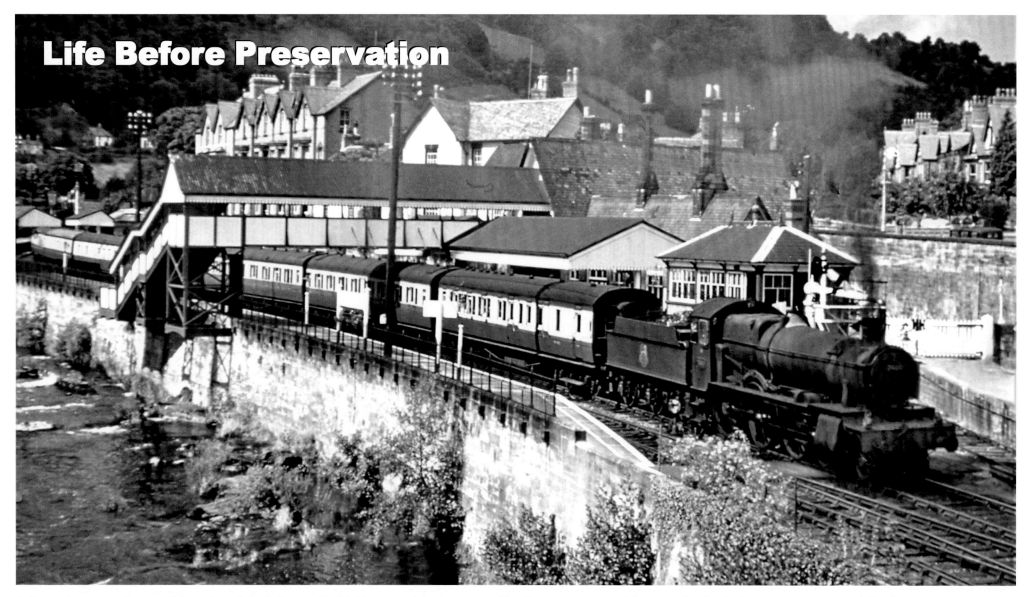

Life Before Preservation

Adorned in a rather grubby plain black livery 7800 Torquay Manor sets off with an up service from Llangollen in May 1953, although the station closed to passenger services on 18 January 1965, it would re-open in preservation on 13 September 1975. Sadly the Manor went for scrap in October 1964, however the Llangollen Railway has continued to prosper as a preserved line ever since. *Colour Rail*

Opposite: Good fortune for both the locomotive and the location, as we see one of Churchward's small prairies 4555 at the head of a returning goods train from Ashburton at Buckfastleigh on 16 November 1960, as both would find their place within the preservation movement. Passenger services along the branch from the mainline at Totnes had finished two years beforehand with the line surviving for goods traffic until 7 September 1962. *Colour Rail*

Opposite: Although a similar scene can be recreated today along the picturesque River Dart, this is how things were in the last summer of passenger operation to Ashburton, with Collett 0-4-2T 1470 barely disturbing the sounds of the magnificent Devon countryside in May 1958. Unfortunately for 1470, although she worked on past closure on goods services and found passenger work elsewhere too, she was sent for scrap in October 1963 to Cashmores in Newport. *Colour Rail*

Another locomotive to be sent for scrap in 1963, was this Collett large prairie 5164, thankfully good fortune stepped in once again as the locomotive went to Woodham's of Barry. She became the 30th escapee from the yard heading to the Severn Valley Railway for sanctuary and restoration in 1973. Meanwhile, Churston station where we see 5164 arriving in the late 1950s would also enjoy a later life within preservation after 1972, between Paignton and Kingswear. *Colour Rail*

Another of Collett's large prairies, 5148 ambles into Kingswear around 1959, just as new DMU services were about to commence, as we can glimpse one lurking in the background. The arrival of these DMUs coincided with a general rundown of services. Goods traffic ceased in 1965, and the track layout was drastically cut back from what we could enjoy in 1958 as 4948 Northwick Hall arrives here at Kingswear. Whereas, 5148 went for scrap back within Swindon Works in the spring of 1960, 4948 worked on until September 1962, before her final scrapping at Cashmore's in Newport in May 1964. *Both: Colour Rail*

The Severn Valley Railway between Kidderminster and Bridgenorth would ultimately be saved by hard working and dedicated preservationists, but on 29 December 1962 this was still the scene at Highley as another large prairie 4153 from 84G Kidderminster shed pauses a while with a duo of brake vans, the tail one being of ex-LNER origin. The station staff have diligently cleared the platform of snow. A second winter visit to the line at Bridgnorth finds another of Kidderminster's allocation on duty with 3601 being held long enough on her passenger turn for a conversation with the crew. *Both: Colour Rail*

Opposite: Once again we are blessed with a happy coincidence, as both the locomotive and location have fallen within the custody of the preservation movement. As we see large prairie 4110 heading away from the stop at Watchet on 18 August 1962 on the line from Taunton to Minehead, much of which would become the West Somerset Railway, five years after closure by British Rail in 1971. While the West Somerset Railway has prospered in preservation, the history of 4110 since being withdrawn in June 1965 has been mixed, as it has yet to steam once again since being the 100th locomotive to be saved from Barry scrapyard. *Colour Rail*

Perhaps one of the most popular locations for steam photographers during the age of Western Region steam, was the stretch of line between Twyford and Woodley just to the east of Reading through the impressive Sonning Cutting. First opened as part of Brunel's broad gauge with just two tracks in 1840, it was widened to the recognizable four tracks of today after the cessation of the broad gauge in 1892. Our first view is from the Bath Road bridge at the western end near Woodley on 27 April 1960, as Britannia 70027 Rising Star heads west with the down Red Dragon for Newport, Cardiff and Swansea. *Colour Rail*

Sonning Salute

Opposite: Down by the line-side to wisely keep our distance, as 4080 Powderham Castle roars past heading west around 1960, just as the Western Region's deliveries of new diesel hydraulics were usurping some of these mainline steam turns. *Colour Rail*

Just a couple of years beforehand on 3 May 1958, the sound of diesel engines within the steep banks of Sonning Cutting was almost unheard of, as a well burnished 6100 Class large prairie heads a smart red liveried rake eastwards toward Paddington. *Colour Rail*

Having just passed an up express within the cutting, Castle Class, 5073 Blenheim heads westwards under clear signals on 22 August 1959.
Colour Rail

On 27 May 1959, 81D Reading's 6161 another of the once commonplace 6100 Class prairies around the London end of the Western Region, canters through with an interesting array of parcels vehicles on the up slow line. *Colour Rail*

The distant signals are off for both the up and down slow lines, as 6126 from 81B Slough brings a down stopper into view, just before the arrival of the DMUs on these services as the 1950s gave way to the 1960s. *Colour Rail*

Opposite: There are two visitors to the small signal box at Woodley as the signalman can be glimpsed standing by his frame, ready to spot the tail lamp at the rear of 4921 Eaton Hall's train as it passes by his box on 11 May 1959. *Colour Rail*

A view back towards the signal box and our cameraman's previous position on 25 May 1957, as 5963 Wimpole Hall from 82D Westbury heads an empty rake of coal wagons towards Reading. *Colour Rail*

With 6809 Burghclere Grange piloting 7917 North Aston Hall, they form a fine sight as they make light work of their eight-coach up express on 3 May 1958. *Colour Rail*

Opposite: A splendid rake of chocolate and cream coaches comprise this morning's up Red Dragon from South Wales on 27 May 1959, headed by 5042 Winchester Castle from 85A Worcester as the sun is high in the sky just after midday. *Colour Rail*

By way of contrast the sun is still low in the sky on 27 January 1959, and has yet to melt the overnight frost still present of the fast lines in the shadows of Sonning Cutting, before 6167 from the 81B Slough allocation runs briskly past towards Paddington. *Colour Rail*

A close run thing for our photographer on 30 April 1960, as a DMU service for Reading can just be made out on the down slow, almost obscured by the white exhaust given off by the rather clean 6909 Frewin Hall with an up goods. If we look towards the up fast line we can see what looks like a Castle Class fast approaching our camera position near Woodley Signal Box. *Colour Rail*

Likewise, the exhaust of an up train can be seen trailing towards the rear of 7010 Avondale Castle's down express, in addition Twyford's goods shed and station are also to be seen in the distance on 5 December 1959. At this point the Collett 4-6-0 had been a longer term resident of 81A Old Oak Common, since entering service after nationalization in 1948. *Colour Rail*

Today's up Capitals United Express looks to have had a few extra coaches added towards the front to take up heavier passenger numbers on 19 April 1958, no matter as Cardiff Canton's Britannia, 70016 Ariel looks to have everything under control.
Colour Rail

Shed Panoramas

An early 1960s visit to Old Oak Common, might have rewarded you with a scene such as this alongside the large double tracked coaling stage, with both Hawksworth and Collett designed panniers on view together with a 6100 prairie tank and 6991 Acton Burnell Hall just managing to get into the picture too.
Colour Rail

The coaling stage here at 84D Leamington was somewhat smaller commensurate with its much reduced allocation of around thirty-locomotives at the time of nationalization, although when this view was recorded in 1963, it had now shrunk to less than twenty, some of its residents were obviously also diesels too. On 9 September this same year, the shed transferred to the London Midland Region's control and assumed their code of 2L. Final closure came on 14 June 1965 with what was left of its allocation passing to 2A Tyseley, itself now no longer part of the Western Region. *Colour Rail*

Right: There are a number of engines stabled outside in the sunshine here at 83G Penzance on 28 May 1961, including 6800 Arlington Grange to the fore on its home shed. *Gerald T. Robinson*

Below: The long footbridge which was the vantage point for many a spotter and cameraman alike here at Cardiff Canton shows up well in this view, with four Standard Class 9Fs and a Jubilee all in the mix around 1960. *Colour Rail*

Our cameraman must have scaled to the top of the water tower here at 81C Southall, in order to gain this impressive view of the yard on 5 May 1965. Steam still outnumbers diesel, but not for much longer we fear as the shed's scrap road can be seen near the top of the picture overlooking the A.E.C. engine and bus works. *Rail Photoprints*

A splendid line up of 'Taffy Tanks' captured on colour film on 6 August 1961, here at Radyr a sub-shed of 88A Cardiff Cathays situated just north of Cardiff on the line to Pontypridd. Sub-sheds such as this avoided the need for locomotives working the Welsh valley lines to return to their principal sheds at the end of their working day. *Rail Online*

The view from the top of the signals on 10 September 1962, just two days after the cessation of through running on the Somerset & Dorset, shows the turntable and former Midland Railway's shed at Bath Green Park now coded 82F, having previously been 71G within the Southern Region before February 1958. *Rail Photoprints*

As our train northwards departs from Oxford on 27 June 1962, who could resist looking back out of the window to see what was on 81F today. Steam working from the rather ramshackle timber shed building here ceased in December 1965, with a diesel stabling point later being built on the site. *Strathwood Library Collection*

A delightful early summer of 1959 view of 82A Bristol Bath Road shed from the city's Temple Meads station, it was taken just as a gleaming Castle Class locomotive adorned with the Bristolian headboard was ready to come off the shed to work perhaps the region's most revered named express connecting with Paddington. *Colour Rail*

Opposite: Bristol also boasted two other sheds, one at 82B St. Phillips Marsh and the other being this the former Midland Railway's establishment at Barrow Road. Formally 22E within the London Midland Region it had become 82E in February 1958. On 17 October 1965, the now preserved 6435 and 1420 were to be the honored guests. *Colour Rail*

Auto Workers

The driver of Oswestry based 1438 looks out from his well kept steed towards the camera, whilst behind him the guard perhaps exchanges a joke about the contents of the pigeon basket on 19 April 1960 having stepped out of his auto-coach during the stop at Overton-on-Dee. *Rail Photoprints*

Opposite: Although certainly not fitted for auto working Collett's 8750 Class pannier, 4650 from 81B Slough has charge of an auto-coach today while working the line from Princes Risborough to the terminus here at Watlington during the line's year of closure to passenger traffic in 1957.
Leslie Nicholson/The Transport Treasury

Opposite: Another non-auto fitted 8750 Class pannier 3600 steps in for the regular 1400 Class on the Moretonhampstead branch train, on a bright March morning in 1958, its fireman gives our cameraman a cheery wave as they run around their auto-coach. *Colour Rail*

Time for a chat among the crew here at Yatton in between workings of their auto-coach to Clevedon in the mid 1950s, meanwhile the ladies having come to town for their shopping talk among themselves as a younger passenger peers out impatiently at the delay. *Colour Rail*

The auto from Aylesbury catches a couple admirers at Princes Risborough as 1440 arrives towing one of the two named auto-coaches in this case Wren on 16 June 1962. Wren is seen to good effect once again, now departing Aylesbury for Princes Risborough in November 1959, this time with 6429 up front. Both 1440 and 6429 were provided for these duties, by 84C Banbury shed. *Both: Colour Rail*

The other named auto coach Thrush shows off its lined maroon livery at Dulverton bringing up the rear of this working to and from Tiverton behind a lined green auto-fitted 1400 Class on 15 November 1962. *Strathwood Library Collection*

Opposite: Wren now finds itself on the Marlow branch at the terminus on 30 April 1960, as both the driver and the guard look upon a busy platform, with two luggage trolleys, a pram and both a motor bike and a push bike, not too mention what looks like a set of drawers minus its actual drawers! *Colour Rail*

The driver of 1419 takes a seat in the shade for a smoke on his pipe at Lostwithiel during a break in the auto services to and from Fowey in July 1957, meanwhile the guard has made use of the luggage trolley to load his part of the coach. *Strathwood Library Collection*

Opposite: One of the top-feed boiler fitted 1400 Class, 1444 based out of 81D Reading, makes a stop at Wargrave on 3 May 1958, whilst working on the Twyford to Henley-on-Thames branch. Note the former Great Western's provision of a ladies room. *Colour Rail*

Thoughtfully composed we can enjoy the passage of 1471, as it propels two auto-coaches on a an Exe Valley local near Bramford Speke during 1961 after some heavy winter rainfall. *Colour Rail*

Opposite: Still in its plain black livery, 1455 from 84C Banbury makes a bit of a fuss at Aylesbury with another auto working from Princes Risborough in the winter of 1961. *Colour Rail*

Opposite: Next we have two auto-coaches being worked conventionally by the non-fitted Collett 8750 Class pannier 3659 provided by 83C Exeter, most likely it is a stand in for the regular 1400 Class perhaps out of action for a boiler washout on this day in May 1963. *Colour Rail*

One young passenger peers out behind the three British Railway's employees here at Ashburton, in October 1958 just a month before the passenger services ceased. The second coach in the other platform was added on for the morning and afternoon school runs. *Colour Rail*

Roaming Around Wales

A somewhat grubby Collett 4575 Class prairie tank from 89C Machynlleth slakes its thirst and takes a shower while working the Pwllheli portion of the up Cambrian Coast Express during 1959. Be careful sir lest you put your pipe out with all that splashing! *Rail Photoprints*

Opposite: In stark contrast Cardiff Canton's Britannia, 70028 Royal Star is well turned out in July 1957, still carrying her original smoke deflector handrails, as she stands on one of the centre roads at Cardiff General ready to be put onto an up express for Paddington. *Colour Rail*

Some attempt to smarten up the front end of Standard Class 4MT mogul 76038 brightens up the scene, as it pilots a Standard Class 4MT 4-6-0 on the Cambrian Coast Express at Talerddig on 20 August 1966. Sadly now long gone, are the days of a burnished Dukedog piloting a gleaming Manor Class here. *Colour Rail*

Opposite: As a young fireman attempts to trim his coal onboard the 1932 Swindon built 5021 Whittington Castle, standing among the lines of locomotives outside at Cardiff Canton on 17 July 1961, we can see that both the standards of cleanliness and the quality of coal supplies are starting to slip away. *Rail Online*

Opposite: The first built of the forty-five strong Swindon Works constructed Standard Class 3MT 2-6-2Ts arrives at Portmadog with a two-coach local which appears to be well supported by passengers on 9 May 1963. *Colour Rail*

Imagine the noise and the drama as this Standard Class 4MT 4-6-0 duo of 75053 and 75063 bark their way to the summit of the climb at Talerddig on this frosty but gloriously sunny autumnal morning on 28 October 1965. *Colour Rail*

Opposite: More signs that the old order did its best to cling on against the tide of change brought about by the creation of British Railways in 1948, firstly as one of the non-auto Collett 5800 Class sits in the bay at Barmouth during the summer of 1958, a decade after nationalization still wearing the former company's colours. Sadly 5801 from 89C Machynlleth, was withdrawn just a couple of months afterwards in September 1958. *Colour Rail*

Another to keep the GWR flag flying was 7428 from 84J Croes Newydd during April 1959, taking water while making a stop at Trawsfynedd, on the former GWR route from Bala to Blaenau Ffestiniog which would close the following year. As for the Collett 7400 Class, 7428 would soldier on still in this livery until withdrawn from 89D Oswestry in October 1962, to be finally broken up by Cashmores of Great Bridge in late 1964. *Colour Rail*

The last working Dean Goods would be 2538, built in August 1897 at Swindon Works, she would go on to manage almost sixty years of service when withdrawn in May 1957. Here she is shunting at Welshpool on 17 May 1956 at the start of her last year in traffic, as an 89A Oswestry engine. Thankfully, classmate 2516 was selected as part of the National Collection and remains on display at Swindon today. *Colour Rail*

The same longevity cannot be claimed by Standard Class 3MT 82031, seen putting on an additional coach at Machynlleth on 24 May 1962, with just four more years left of its all too short, twelve-year service career still to go. Withdrawn from 9H Patricroft in December 1966, she hung around from May 1967 in Cashmore's Newport scrapyard until finally cut up there in October 1968. *Colour Rail*

Opposite: Making its way gracefully away from the speed restriction across Barmouth Bridge and into the town around 1958 is 9004, one of the then eight surviving outside-framed Dukedog 4-4-0s rebuilt and created between 1931 and 1939 from the earlier Dean designed engines from 1903 to 1906. *Colour Rail*

Another case of old and almost new in the early 1960s at Talerddig, as Standard Class 2MT mogul 78005, dating from February 1953, pilots one of Churchward's moguls 6356 built in November 1923 towards the summit of this steep climb, with stretches at 1 in 52! The nearby station closed in 1968, although the line still remains open. *Colour Rail*

Opposite: On 29 December 1965, the overnight frost is beginning to clear by the time the Standard Class 4MT 4-6-0 duo of 75053 and 75063 pass Carno with the Cambrian Coast Express. The fireman from both locomotives have steam to spare on their charges, so they hang out of the their respective cabs to enjoy the day. *Colour Rail*

The level crossing gates have clattered shut, thus preventing these pedestrians from delaying the departure of this 87E Landore allocated Fowler Class 4MT from Pontardulais in June 1960, with a local stopper. Note how the once bright crimson livery of the leading coach has faded badly. *Colour Rail*

On 19 April 1962, the fireman of 5961 Toynbee Hall looks on, as two porters collect up some more luggage trolleys at Cardiff General. One wonders if they had to clear off some spotters from these trollies first, surely it has happened to all of us at one time or another while in pursuit of our hobby as youngsters? *Colour Rail*

The spruced up 75056 leads a fellow Standard Class 4MT 4-6-0 away from Llandbrynmair on 20 August 1966 with today's Cambrian Coast Express. Eighty of these fine locomotives were built at Swindon Works between 1951 and 1956, by the close of 1966 their numbers would be down to forty-nine left in service. *Colour Rail*

Opposite: Several of the Western Region's allocation of Standard Class 4MT 4-6-0s carried the lined green livery courtesy of overhauls back at Swindon or sometimes also at Eastleigh Works. The mail and parcels are still being unloaded here at Morfa Mawddach on 3 June 1966, but the guard has his green flag at the ready to signal to the fireman around the adverse curve of the platform and will no doubt quickly jump back aboard, leaving a peaceful feeling back across the station once more. *Colour Rail*

With just three coaches behind 7819 Hinton Manor her crew can easily accelerate past the mainline engine shed from their standing start at Aberystwyth on 23 December 1963, perhaps its an early beginning for their Christmas spirit. The Manor was withdrawn in November 1965 and sent to Barry Scrapyard in early 1966, before being rescued for preservation in 1973 with much work for the volunteers at the Severn Valley Railway still to complete, but she was back in steam again during 1977. *Colour Rail*

Opposite: One of the earliest lined green repaints for the Swindon built Standard Class 3MTs was to 82003, here she is making a steamy departure with just a single coach from Llanbrynmair several years later in August 1964, just passing the tablet catcher. *Colour Rail*

Making their third appearance together on Cambrian Coast Express duty are the pairing of Standard Class 4MT 4-6-0s 75053 and 75063. This time there looks to be little chance of the frost clearing as they pass Abermule on 28 December 1965. *Colour Rail*

Perhaps a case of little and large with these two views, in this first one, the diminutive Powlesland & Mason 0-4-0ST 1152, makes its way through the backstreets around Swansea Docks in September 1959. There are so many things to enjoy once again in this period piece as the gentleman in the raincoat stands by the entrance to the tiny cafe and the barbershop. In this second view the short-lived Standard Class 9F 92216 is being pushed out further into the shed yard by the Castle Class locomotive behind at Cardiff Canton in August 1962. Built at Swindon in December 1959, 92216 would be withdrawn before she was just six years old in October 1965, what a waste of resources! *Both: Colour Rail*

Well prepared for top link work outside its home shed of 87E Landore in 1959 is 7009 Athenley Castle, nine years into its slightly longer fifteen-year working career. *Colour Rail*

Dukedog 9024 holds up the traffic, as she leaves Fairbourne in June 1954 with a local service. Including its original form when built in April 1904, this graceful locomotive lasted fifty-three years in service until withdrawn in August 1957. *Colour Rail*

With a set of fire irons discarded alongside the ground signal it appears this grubby lined green Standard Class 3MT will soon be making its way off shed at Machynlleth in September 1963. The shed here had been coded 89C until the 9th of this month then it became 6F within the London Midland Region until complete closure came on 5 December 1966. *Colour Rail*

A respectfully clean Camping Coach greets the arrival of another grubby lined green locomotive in the shape of Churchward prairie 4569 into Tenby from Whitland in August 1962. All seventy-five of these locomotives made it into British Railways' ownership in 1948, but by the close of 1962 just six remained in service. *Colour Rail*

The twenty locomotives within Collett's non-auto fitted 5800 Class all lasted until 1957, when eleven of their number were withdrawn including 5811, seen here at Manod near Blaenau Ffestiniog in August 1955. *Colour Rail*

In May 1956, the coal traffic appears to be buoyant here at Castle Caerinion on the Welshpool & Llanfair narrow gauge, as six coal-men start to clear this freshly delivered load. Meanwhile, 822 once named The Earl was still to be seen in use shunting the yard. There were two of these 0-6-0T locomotives built for this 2' 9" narrow gauge line in September 1902, the other 823 once named The Countess was the first to be stored when freight working declined the following year after this photograph was taken. Both locomotives can be seen today on the preserved section of the line. *Colour Rail*

There were three other other narrow gauge 2' 6" locomotives to survive after British Railways closed the Corris Railway in 1948, these were on the Vale of Rheidol line. Here we have 8 Llywelyn making a rousing sight passing their own original narrow gauge engine shed at Aberystwyth, where 7 Owain Glyndwr can just be glimpsed on 3 July 1965. The third locomotive, 9 Prince of Wales poses alongside the standard gauge station at Aberystwyth on 20 May 1961.
Both: Colour Rail

Opposite: A reminder that Collett's 6100 Class did not all work exclusively within the London Division of the Western Region, as we see a well kept 6108 sitting quietly in the sunshine at 88B Radyr, its then home shed on 6 August 1961. It would however retire back to 81E Didcot that November to see out its days until August 1965 once more closer to Paddington. *Rail Online*

The two station staff and a visiting Post Office worker pose for the camera here at Llanfrynach on 25 May 1963. The engine crew of 4569 making its second appearance in this book are shrouded in steam on this delightfully crisp spring morning to enjoy working in the countryside. *Colour Rail*

Opposite: This smartly attired Collett 5600 Class locomotive not only carries the luxury of a lined green livery but also a train reporting number frame when captured at Ebbw Junction on 12 July 1959. The 86H shed plate correctly denotes its allocation to Aberbeeg shed at this time. *Colour Rail*

The close proximity for access to the engine shed here at Machynlleth is well seen from the hillside overlooking the station on 20 August 1966, while the lined green liveried Standard Class 4MT 4-6-0, 75002 makes another appearance this time working a Pwlhelli to Paddington service. *Colour Rail*

Preparing his engine for the day ahead, the fireman on the footplate is oblivious to our cameraman here at Rhymney on 16 April 1960. Recently through works judging by its condition, 5662 remained at this shed from October 1948 until it was withdrawn in November 1964. It was then noted dumped at 88D Merthyr shed for a short while before being taken into the scrapyard of R.S. Hayes Ltd at Bridgend and swiftly broken up by mid-January 1965. *Colour Rail*

On 4 March 1967, photographers seize their chances to record the last scheduled steam haulage for the Cambrian Coast Express during a stop at Newtown, while staff hastily deal with the parcels traffic onboard today. Standard Class 4MT 4-6-0 75021 carries a wreath on its coupling hook and although externally filthy, some attempt has been made to clean up the smokebox area. Very soon 75021 would be transferred to 10A Carnforth to see out its short career until withdrawn in February the following year. *Colour Rail*

Specials

On 25 July 1965, this jointly run LCGB & REC tour started the day behind Class 2MT mogul 46509 out of Waterloo before taking a circuitous route to reach Kensington Olympia and the Western Region, where 6106 seen here later on at Hanwell along with pannier tank 9773 would share the work to take in former steam branch routes, such as Greenford, Brentford, Staines West, Windsor & Eton Central and Henley-on-Thames before a handover to Class 4MT 80154 at Reading for a return via LSWR metals to Waterloo once more. With the Great Western Society's headboard in place on 20 September 1964 at Westbury, this Collett 1400 Class takes in the sunshine while working a special around Wiltshire to help them to raise funds for preservation, from little acorns as they say.

Photos: Strathwood Library Collection & Colour Rail

The East Midlands branch of the RCTS organized a tour on 6 May 1956 from Nottingham Midland down to Swindon Works utilizing two ex-Midland Railway Johnson/Fowler Class 2P 4-4-0s. One was 40489, the other 40454 is seen here being turned within the works where the tour participants enjoyed a conducted visit around the once extensive workshops. Looking on is the recently withdrawn Taff Vale 0-6-2T 382 which saw very brief use finally as a works shunter before being scrapped here that September. *Colour Rail*

Another Midland Railway connection is made here at Oxford on 11 September 1960, as the preserved Class 4P Compound 1000 hands over to Churchward mogul 7317 for the run down to Eastleigh Works with the RCTS East Midlander No.4 Rail Tour. *Colour Rail*

Two Gresley designed interlopers next on Western Region rail tours, firstly with the late Alan Peglar's Flying Scotsman running only on two-cylinders, the near-side one had blown out a packing gland as and was just about useless, but still going well with the Panda Pullman passing Hanwell on 13 November 1965. Then we see 60007 Sir Nigel Gresley at High Wycombe a few weeks beforehand on 23 October with the A4 Preservation Society's Paddington Streamliner tour. *Photos: Aldo Delicata & Colour Rail*

The spark arresting chimney does little for the looks of 2144, a Dean designed pannier tank built at Wolverhampton Works in May 1904, as they attempt to take water at Cleobury Mortimer on 21 May 1955. The tour was most likely this venerable locomotive's last duty as she was withdrawn the same month. *Colour Rail*

Opposite: Water is being taken by this Collett 0-4-2T during a stop at Kemble on 6 April 1964, as the Gloucestershire Railway Society made one last steam tour to visit both the Cirencester Town and the Tetbury branches. With 1472 being used throughout, and back and forth from Gloucester Central too it is no wonder she was in need of a drink. *Colour Rail*

One for the number spotters perhaps as Collett's prairie 5555 and 2251 Class, 2222 stand at Towyn on 30 September 1961 with a Talyllyn Railway Society special. *Gerald T. Robinson*

Approaching Churchill Crossing between Kingham & Chipping Norton on 14 September 1963, Collett prairie 6111 has an easy enough task working the Railway Enthusiasts' Club tour named The Chiltern 200. *Strathwood Library Collection*

On 3 June 1961, 1363 one of the last two Churchward 1361 Class still remaining in service was used for a tour around Plymouth including the Sutton Harbour Branch, arranged by the Plymouth Railway Circle.
Strathwood Library Collection

A chance for a closer look at one of the surviving Dukedogs 9021, during a water stop at Welshpool on 28 September 1957 while it was being piloted by 50781, an ex-LNWR Aspinall Class 2P. The pair worked the Shrewsbury to Towyn leg of their then annual Talyllyn Railway Preservation Society's AGM special from Paddington for members. *Colour Rail*

The crudely lined out green livery that Britannia 70004 formally named William Shakespeare wears here, did little for its latter day appearance in comparison with its earlier days working the Golden Arrow from Stewarts Lane shed! However, it stood in for one of the legs that 60532 Blue Peter was due to complete on 14 August 1966 on this LCGB special, and unlike the A2 is seen here with steam to spare at Westbury. *Colour Rail*

Using the former Stratford-upon-Avon and Midland Junction Railway's connection at Woodford Halse on 12 October 1963, this pairing of 6368 and 2246 head the LCGB's Thames, Avon and Severn Railtour towards Worcester. *Rail Photoprints*

Everyone seems wrapped up for the cold, even to take 16mm cine footage from one gentleman with his beret on here at Monmouth Troy, the headboard on 6412 tells the sad tale. *Colour Rail*

LAST TRAIN
MONMOUTH
—ROSS
4TH JAN.1959

·6412·

Today's driver who is obscured by the Bristol Bath Road shed-master onboard 5054 Earl of Ducie, has proudly affixed his brass driver's name plaque to the cabside. These were a nice touch showing the pride of the former GWR and Western Region that fell out of use, even though provision was made for them on many of the new diesel hydraulics too. This Castle Class locomotive was one of four chosen for 9 May 1964, to work the Ian Allan, Great Western High Speed Railtour. The Western Region went to a huge amount of effort to make this tour a success, it was to be the swansong of Great Western steam. Nothing was left to chance. The remaining Castle Class locomotives were carefully put through their paces and the best ones, 4079 Pendennis Castle, 5054 Earl of Ducie, 7025 Sudeley Castle and 7029 Clun Castle were all chosen prior to the trip. Standby Castles were stationed at all key points and specially selected best Welsh coal was provided for the tour's locomotives, which were thoroughly prepared with boilers washed out and tender water tanks cleaned, with two firemen being employed on each locomotive. Sadly, this choice of high quality, very hot burning coal together with the high rate of firing is likely to have contributed to 4079's failure, as her firebars failed, leading to its substitution at Westbury by 6999 Capel Dewi Hall which put a small damper upon this notable day. *Colour Rail*

As this was to be the last scheduled steam haulage of the 16.15 Paddington to Banbury on 11 June 1965, 7029 Clun Castle was duly rostered and dressed appropriately, with the Great Western Railways coat of arms as it called here at Princes Risborough. No doubt all the windows were duly taken by enthusiasts anxious to savor what might be their last runs behind a Castle or so they though back then. *Colour Rail*

Opposite: The unusual appearance of 89C Machynlleth allocated Dukedog 9017, seen here taking water at Oxford on 20 April 1958, came about as a result of the Railway Enthusiast Club's Severn Rambler tour which it ran in connection with Collett 5400 Class pannier 5417 using two short rakes of coaches. *Colour Rail*

There was a good turn out for the Great Western Society's Cookham Manor Railtour and Open Day at Taplow on 17 September 1966, a year after steam had officially ceased on the Western Region. For the Open Day here alongside the mainline in the goods yard, Old Oak Common provided several diesel hydraulics and their cinema coach, while the society's now preserved Collett prairie 6106 was booked to be giving ½ mile rides pulling their Ocean Saloon (no. 9118). Special fares were available from many locations, all using service trains, to get to Taplow, in addition 4079 Pendennis Castle and the preserved Collett 2251 Class 3205 were also here on display. *Rail Online*

To celebrate exactly one hundred years to the day after the opening of Brunel's Royal Albert Bridge at Saltash, the RCTS arranged for this seven-coach special headed on the down direction to Plymouth by 7001 Sir James Milne, we catch our view here near Reading West just before 09.30. The return run was made appropriately behind another Castle, 5069 Isambard Kingdom Brunel, arriving back at Paddington at 22.30. In between times, ticket holders enjoyed an extensive tour around the Plymouth area using 6420 and 30182. *Colour Rail*

Opposite: The Stephenson Locomotive Society ran an enterprising tour on 13 May 1961, out and back from Gloucester Central, as their Severn & Wye District Tour. What made it so interesting was the use of just three auto-coaches and two locomotives to avoid the problems of running around. As some of the locations visited were by this stage problematic. Auto-fitted Collett pannier tank 6437 was sandwiched inside the train between two and remaining one of the auto-coaches, with 8701 seen here added on later in the day as we catch up with the tour at Coleford. *Colour Rail*

A very popular tour was run on 9 May 1964, starting out from Nottingham Victoria, with 46251 City of Nottingham working as far as Didcot where 34038 Lynton took over for the run to Eastleigh. Here USA tank 30071, took the train into the works for a full visit, then a return was made by the Bulleid Pacific here to Swindon Works where this magnificent Stanier Pacific was waiting at the engine shed for the return to Nottingham after another full works tour. Perhaps less glamorous was the Swansea Railway Circle's tour on 31 July 1965, using Collett 5600 Class, 6643 throughout as their Rambling 56 Railtour, a brief stop for water was made here at Bargoed. *Photos:* **Strathwood Library Collection & Colour Rail**

Somerset & Dorset Recalled

Opposite: With closure of the line set for the next day on 6 March 1966, we capture Stanier Class 8F 48706, having stopped for water at Evercreech Junction with a Great Western Society arranged commemorative tour. The Bath Green Park allocated Class 8F was withdrawn two days after this view on 7 March and after a short period of storage found its way to Buttigieg's scrapyard in Newport on 6 April 1966. *Tony Butcher*

Twelve years beforehand there was no hint of the Somerset & Dorset's demise as we see this Ian Allan - Trains Illustrated arranged excursion, coming off Prestleigh Viaduct on 25 April 1954. It has Class 2P 40601 providing the tablet catching apparatus for the train tucked in behind Maunsell's Schools Class, 30932 Blundells. Originally it was planned to to have a Drummond Class T9 fitted as the tablet catcher locomotive for the tour which came to naught. *Colour Rail*

A busy morning at Bath Green Park shed on 5 March 1966, as these two bulled up Bulleid pacifics are being prepared for their part in what were four specials run over the Somerset & Dorset that final weekend. When the pair go off shed 34006 Bude will lead 34057 Biggin Hill, as they run double-headed to Evercreech Junction to meet their train. This is how we would prefer to remember the Somerset & Dorset with Standard Class 4MT 75023 piloting Bulleid pacific 34043 Combe Martin on the up Pines Express off the single line at Midford, in the summer of 1962.

Photos: George Woods & Colour Rail

Having been brought to Bath Green Park shed in July 1962, specifically for working the last running of the Pines Express along the Somerset & Dorset, before it was re-routed via Oxford after 8 September 1962. Two days later, we see her in steam back on 82F Bath Green Park awaiting her next duty before being re-allocated to 81A Old Oak Common. *Rail Photoprints*

Opposite: Another lined green British Railways Standard on the route at this time, was this Class 4MT 75027, based out of 72G Templecombe. In this scene taken at Evercreech Junction on 17 August 1962 as a young fireman sees her head off once again, it must be said she could have done with a good clean! *Colour Rail*

Time for a chat on 1 September 1962 at Evercreech Junction, perhaps about who might be rostered for the last workings of the Pines Express on the 8th of the month. *Colour Rail*

The noisy Peak is held at the signals as 34042 Wilton heads away from Bath Green Park with a relief portion to the Pines Express bound for Bournemouth West. Then D124 will back down to Green Park station, in order to take over a northbound service for the Midlands on 9 June 1962. *Rail Photoprints*

Winter often on the Somerset & Dorset was a quieter time without all of the holiday trains, but nethertheless a good time to be out watching the passage of what was running while you still could. As here on 28 December 1965, with Standard Class 4MT 4-6-0, 75072 crossing the River Stour at Sturminster Newton as it heads the 11.45 Bournemouth to Bristol Temple Meads service. Having left the narrow confines of Devonshire Tunnel, Standard Class 5MT, 73054 climbs through Lyncombe Vale with the 09.03 Bristol Temple Meads to Bournemouth West service, on 6 March 1965 exactly a year before closure. *Both: Rail Photoprints*

Fellow cameramen stand at the platform end for their going away shots as Somerset & Dorset Class 7F, 53809 pilots un-rebuilt West Country pacific 34103 Calstock away from Evercreech Junction with both engines blowing off on this summer Saturday service from Bournemouth to the North over this once much loved route on 1 September 1962. *Rail Photoprints*

Opposite: Enthusiasts and sightseers gather at Highbridge on 5 March 1966 during that last weekend of working, as they await fellow Ivatt Class 2MT 41307 to back onto 41249, in order that the pair may work the LCGB's special back to Evercreech Junction and to meet up with the waiting pair of Bulleids we have already seen on page 144. *Colour Rail*

With the last through running of the Pines Express over the Somerset & Dorset already publicized, many photographers headed to the line to record things for themselves, before it was too late. One such visitor once again on 1 September 1962, was on hand here at Shepton Mallet to witness the passing of Standard Class 9F, 92001 at the head of a Bradford to Bournemouth through train. Re-allocated back to 82F Bath Green Park for the second summer season in a row from her winter duties out of 88A Cardiff Canton, soon this fine Class 9F would leave the Somerset & Dorset for good within days to take up residence next at 81F Oxford. *Rail Photoprints*

From an elevated viewpoint we see Standard Class 4MT 4-6-0, 75073 approaching Templecombe's upper station with a Somerset & Dorset line local on 4 August 1962. *Rail Photoprints*

An unusual sight at Templecombe shed on 28 March 1965, as rebuilt Merchant Navy pacific 35023 Holland Africa Line waits for the returning Southern Counties Touring Society's excursion covering part of the Somerset & Dorset. The highlight for some was the run back from here at Templecombe to Wimbledon on the return to London Victoria, this was booked for 105 minutes for the 105 miles. Although there was only a light load of just seven coaches, after a late start from Templecombe they arrived back at Wimbledon in just over 95 minutes, despite three signal checks en-route. Hardly likely to match this kind of performance was this Fowler Class 4F, as 44560 climbs away from Midford with the 15.20 Bath Green Park to Templecombe service, on 28 April 1962. This locomotive was one of five ordered for the Somerset & Dorset and built to the original Midland design by Armstrong Whitworth in 1922. *Both: Rail Photoprints*

158

One of the Somerset & Dorset's very own Class 7F 2-8-0s, 53808 passes Midsomer Norton South with today's, Nottingham to Bournemouth Saturdays only service on 4 August 1962. Following on from page 153 we can see that Ivatt Class 2MT 41307 was in the lead of 41249 on the LCGB's special as her crew look back along their train at Glastonbury on 5 March 1966. *Photos: Rail Photoprints & George Woods*

One last look back to recall Class 9F 92220 Evening Star during her brief transfer to the Somerset & Dorset. Once more on 1 September 1962, she is seen at Templecombe waiting for the signal on her southbound journey having just been dragged down from Templecombe's upper station back onto S & D metals, the train is the 09.03 Bristol Temple Meads to Bournemouth West. *Rail Photoprints*